CUSTODIAL TORTURE IN INDIA: NEED FOR SEPARATE LEGISLATION

VOLUME 2, ISSUE 3 OF BRILLOPEDIA

RAHUL SK

Contents

Preface

"Start writing, no matter what. The water does not flow until the faucet is turned on".

• Louis L'Amour

Hundreds of students and professors are contributing their work to Brillopedia, we are here to provide ample information about Law and Contemporary issues. Our aim is to provide a platform for today's generation to express their views and ideas on law and contemporary law.

Author

Rahul SK

Publication

This research paper is published in volume 2, issue 3 of Brillopedia

CHAPTER ONE

ABSTRACT

Torture, as a crime is universally accepted and agreed by the civilized nations, as the crime against humanity. It has become the part of the customary international law. India however is the party to the Convention against Torture, but it is yet to enact any municipal law protecting and preventing its citizens from torture. The paper discusses the inhumane prison conditions in India, custodial torture, and torture during police investigations. We have seen in recent times how, by not having the torture law has proved to be a greater impediment in bringing back the criminals from foreign territories (Extradition). There is a detailed discussion on international perspective; the comparative study of multiple jurisdictions, where the torture law is already the part of their municipal law. It also discusses the approach of the Indian Supreme Court vis-à-vis torture. The aim of this paper is to bring in light, the need and importance of torture law in India. The law against torture is the essential requirement to uphold the constitutional culture, essentially meant for the dignity of individuals. The international norms require that, the law against torture should be the part of domestic legislation. Last, but not the least the paper advocates for the separate legislation on torture, which is evident from the conclusion and suggestions given in the paper.

Keywords: Custodian Torture, BRICS, Citizens, India, Legislation, International Law, Humanity

CHAPTER TWO

INTRODUCTION

Torture is the most important problem in this third world, and it is considered as the worldwide phenomenon inflicted upon the individuals irrespective of age, sex, and health condition. However, freedom from torture is one of the most universally recognized human rights, still there are torture in almost all countries in the world. If we talk about the custodial torture then also it is existed in almost all the country in the world. It is an important weapon in the hands of police and investigating agencies to compel the person to tell lie. It is worst violation of human rights. Mostly the torture is perpetuated by the police, jail authorities, armed forces and other law enforcing agencies. In the present day hardly, a week passes without an incident of custodial torture or custodial death.

India is the biggest democracy in the world, and since it has the diversity of religion, culture, practice, custom etc., here it is very easy to commit torture against a person. Though a person may not be a police officer or jail authorities but still he can commit torture by saying any obscene word or by insulting any person on the basis of caste. There is law relating to this i.e., SC/ST Prevention of Atrocities Act, 1989 which prohibit any comment to any SC/ST regarding their caste, and if committed then that will be treated as the torture. In custodial torture India's position is very bad, since there is end number of examples of custodial death due to the torture in the police or judicial custody which is reported. It means there are also cases which are not reported rather remain unreported. In most of the time the victims of the torture are economically poor, socially deprived sections of our society. Reasons for being a victim of torture are power, position and money. Those who are having one of these three things can never be subjected to torture.

In the present-day custodial torture is the common problem for almost all the country in the world. However, happenings of torture are increasing day by day. As per the Amnesty[1] report 2017-2018 between January and

August 2018, number of deaths in judicial custody is 894 and death in police custody is 74. As per the NHRC[2] report number of custodial death in judicial custody is 1636 and in police custody is 148. NHRC recommended for monetary relief to the family of victims. As per the same report large number of cases of torture is with the state of Uttar Pradesh. Asian Centre for Human Rights (ACHR) reported that India recorded five custodial deaths per day on an average between April 2017 and February 2018.[3]

[1]Amnesty International, Amnesty International Report, Amnesty International (Aug 20, 2022)https://www.amnestyusa.org/wp-content/uploads/2018/02/POL1067002018ENGLISH.pdf.

[2] NHRC,*Annual Report2018-2019*, NHRC (Sept 12, 2022)https://nhrc.nic.in/sites/default/files/Annual%20Report%202018-29_final.pdf.

[3]Sankalita Dey,*In 2017-18, there were 5 custodial deaths per day in India*, the Print(Sept 12, 2022) https://theprint.in/india/governance/in-2017-18-there-were-5-custodial-deaths-per-day-in-india-says-report/75654/

CHAPTER THREE

TORTURE: MEANING

Torture is the deliberate infliction of physical or mental suffering by one person to another. In other word we can say it is the act by one person against other against his/her will. It may be noted that torture is always by the person having authority over the victim, for example police having authority over the accused person and jail authority having the authority over the prisoners.

Oxford English dictionary defined torture as "The action or practice of inflicting severe pain on someone as a punishment or in order to force them to do or say something."

As per the **Merriam Webster dictionary** torture means, "the act of causing several physical pains as a form of punishment or as a way to force someone to do or say something"

Article 1 of the **Convention Against Torture, 1984**[1] defined torture as " any act by which severe pain or suffering, whether physical or mental, is intentionally inflicted on a person for such purposes as obtaining from him or a third person information or a confession, punishing him for an act he or a third person has committed or is suspected of having committed, or intimidating or coercing him or a third person, or for any reason based on discrimination of any kind, when such pain or suffering is inflicted by or at the instigation of or with the consent or acquiescence of a public official or other person acting in an official capacity. It does not include pain or suffering arising only from, inherent in or incidental to lawful sanctions."

A bill was introduced in the Indian Parliament in 2010[2], but unfortunately it was not passed, the proposed definition in that bill defined torture as "Whoever, being a public servant or being abetted by a public servant or with the consent or acquiescence of a public servant, intentionally does any act for the purposes to obtain from him or a third person such information or a confession which causes, —

(*i*) Grievous hurt to any person; or

(*ii*) Danger to life, limb or health (whether mental or physical) of any person, is said to inflict torture:

Provided that nothing contained in this section shall apply to any pain, hurt or danger as aforementioned caused by any act, which is inflicted in accordance with any procedure established by law or justified by law."

[1]Convention against Torture and Other Cruel, Inhuman or Degrading Treatment or Punishment, Adopted and opened for signature, ratification and accession by General Assembly resolution 39/46 of 10 December 1984 (entry into force 26 June 1987), in the same way, Article 7(2)(e) of The Rome Statute of the International Criminal Court, (A/CONF.183/9) define the term torture. It says that torture means the intentional infliction of severe pain or suffering, whether physical or mental, upon a person in the custody or under the control of the accused; except that torture shall not include pain or suffering arising only from, inherent or incidental to, lawful sanctions.

[2] Prevention of Torture Bill, 2010, No. 58, Bill of Parliament, 2010 (India).

CHAPTER FOUR

TORTURE LAW: AN INTERNATIONAL PROSPECTIVE

If we talk about the torture law in international prospective then we may find various initiatives which are taken by the United Nations and General Assembly. At the international level there is enough number of torture laws are there and we can divide it into four categories, Torture law at universal level, torture law at regional level, United Nations Protocols and guidelines regarding prevention of torture and commentaries by committee against torture. At the universal level Article 5 of the Universal Declaration of Human Rights prohibits torture and provides that No one shall be subjected to torture or to cruel, inhuman or degrading treatment or punishment.[1] Article 7 of the ICCPR prohibit torture and provides that No one shall be subjected to torture or to cruel, inhuman or degrading treatment or punishment. In particular, no one shall be subjected without his free consent to medical or scientific experimentation.[2] UN Convention Against Torture,[3] UN Optional Protocol,[4] Rome Statute of International Criminal Court,[5]UN Declaration on Torture[6]. At the regional level there are various legal framework on torture such as Article 5 of the American Convention on Human Rights which is also known as Pact of San Jose, Inter American Convention to Prevent and Punish Torture, Article 3 of the European Convention on Human Rights and Article 5 of the African Charter on People's and Human Rights provides for the prevention and punishment for torture.

3.1. Initiatives taken by the United Nations: The United Nations has played a key role in prevention of custodial violence including torture and to secure custodial justice. The United Nations since its formation has been providing standard and practices by introducing various international instruments such as UDHR 1948, ICCPR 1966, UN Convention Against Torture and Other Cruel, in Human and Degrading Treatment and Punishment (CAT 1984), the United Nations Basic Principles of Justice for Victim of Crimes and Abuse of Power (UNBPVC1985), the United Nations Optional Protocol of Convention Against Torture and Other Cruel, Human and Degrading Treatment and Punishment (OPCAT 2006) and International Convention for the Protection of all Persons from Enforced Disappearance (ICPED 2007), the United Nations Standard Minimum Rules for Treatment of Offenders, 1955, United Nations Code of Conduct for Law Enforcement Officials, 1979, the United Nations Minimum Rules for non-Custodial Measures(the Tokyo Rules), the United Nations body Principles for Protection of all Persons from any forms of Detention or Imprisonment, and the United Nations Basic Principles on use of Force and Firearms for Law Enforcement Officials 1991.[7]

3.2. United Nations Bodies and Mechanism regarding torture: The United Nations has established various Committees, bodies, special Reporter etc. to monitor of human rights standards at domestic level such as

- UN Human Rights Committee
- UN High Commissioner for Human Rights
- UN Committee Against Torture
- UN Subcommittee on Prevention of Torture
- UN Special Reporter on Torture
- UN Voluntary Fund for Victims of Torture
- UN International Day for Victims of Victims of Torture on 26th Jun

[1] Universal Declaration of Human Rights, 1948(10th Dec 1948 as resolution No 217 by UN General Assembly).

[2] International Covenant on Economic, Social and Cultural Rights, 1966 (Resolution No 2200A, XXI on 16th Dec. 1966, w.e.f. 23rd March 1976).

[3]Convention against Torture and Other Cruel, Inhuman or Degrading Treatment or Punishment, Adopted and opened for signature, ratification and accession by General Assembly resolution 39/46 of 10 December 1984 (entry into force 26 June 1987).

[4]Optional Protocol to the Convention against Torture and other Cruel, Inhuman or Degrading Treatment or Punishment, 2002 (Passed on 18th Dec 2002 at 57th session of GA by Resolution No A/RES/57/199, Entry into force 22nd June 2006).

[5]Article 7(2) (e) of The Rome Statute of the International Criminal Court, (A/CONF.183/9) define the term torture. It says that torture means the intentional infliction of severe pain or suffering, whether physical or mental, upon a person in the custody or under the control of the accused; except that torture shall not include pain or suffering arising only from, inherent or incidental to, lawful sanctions.

[6] General Assembly on December 9, 1975 adopted a Declaration on the Protection of All Persons from Being Subjected to Torture and other Cruel, Inhuman or Degrading Treatment or Punishment, (Mar 29, 2022) https://www.ohchr.org/en/instruments-mechanisms/instruments/ declaration-protection-all-persons-being-subjected-torture-and

[7] Chakraborty, Law on Custodial death and Torture 54(First Edition, 2017).

CHAPTER FIVE

TORTURE LAW AND INDIA

In India, there are two types custody, one is police custody and another is judicial custody. In most of the time torture happened in police custody, the police misuse their power and creating the fear in the mind of the general people.

Law in all countries authorizes the police to use force under stances. This authority is, in fact, basic to its role and cannot a part of policeman's legal mandate. The police have to protect the acts of murderers, armed robbers, habitual criminals, arsonists and make it a safe place to live in. Thus, apprehension of the gang of an accused, who violently defies arrest, etc., are the situations measure of counter violence by the police. But the police have certainly no right to inflict brutality on under its custody ignoring every law of the land. In a democratic people and not the police are the real masters as the sovereign power them. The police are simply the agent of the government which accountable to the people. So, the police too are accountable their acts.[1]

The code of conduct for police in India, adopted at the Conference of Inspector - Generals of Police in 1960 also deals with this issue. Clause, I state that the police must bear faithful allegiance to the Constitution of India and respect and uphold the rights of the citizens as guaranteed by it. Clause 2 states that the police are essentially a law enforcement agency, and it should not usurp the function of judiciary and sit in judgment on cases. Clause 3 states that under no circumstances should it punish the guilty which is the function of judiciary. But in India, the police lack the sense of accountability. There is growing tendency on the part of police to act unlawfully. The result is horrifying cases of brutal custodial torture.[2]

Death as a result of torture in police custody is indeed one of worst kinds of crime in a society governed by rule of law that promises to secure to all its citizens, amongst others, justice, liberty and equality. Such cases not only pose serious threat to the orderly civilized society but also are an affront to human dignity.[3]

5.1. History of Torture and measures taken by: The phenomenon of custodial torture is not new in India. India had witnessed the torture and violence by the police from the very beginning i.e., from the Vedic age (2000-1400 B.C.). The ordeals of fire and single combat were used. In the Epic period (1400-800 B.C.) torture was practiced on prisoners by the police. Torture in various forms was widely prevalent in the age of laws and philosophy (800-320 B.C.). *Kautilya'sArthashastra* speaks about various kinds of torture such as burning of limbs, tearing by wild animals, tramping to death by elephants and bull, cutting of limb and mutilation etc. Manu the law giver in that age opined in favor of having the torture to protect the society from the criminals. Buddhist period (300 B.C.-300 A.D.) was an age of great humanitarianism and administration of justice. Torture in any form was strictly prohibited. Under the Mughals no criminal and civil code existed. Torture to extort confession was widely spread.[4]

In the British period, the torture was used by the official including Kotwals resulting death sooner or after. In 1855 a Torture Commission was set up by the British Government in Madras Presidency, in its report committee submitted that police torture was quite prevalent in the Madras Presidency. This commission defined the term torture and in 1860 Police Commission was set up as a consequence of that commission. Then in 1861 police Act passed and torture law governed. After independence, several Police Commissions were appointed by the Union and State Governments to look into the early 1970 and 1980. Commissions established in various state including Kerala[5], Punjab[6], Bihar[7], West Bengal[8], Maharashtra[9], Madhya Pradesh[10], Delhi[11], Tamil Nadu[12], and Assam[13]. Central Government also appointed two commissions[14].

During the emergency from 1975 to 1977 there was police brutality in wide range[15]. National Police Commission, 1979 recommended the Government to take the measures to insulate the police from illegitimate political and executive interference. There should be mandatory judicial inquiry in cases of deaths and rapes in police custody.

5.2. Legal regime and efforts on Torture: In India we may found only some laws related to torture, which directly or indirectly deals with torture not in single document but in various documents. Although such provisions are not strong in itself, and misuse of such provisions are common by the police.

5.2.1. under the constitution:there are three Articles directly and indirectly related to torture such as 20, 21 and 22. Article 20(1) provides for prohibition of retrospective operation of penal legislation, which is also a kind of torture and cruelty against the human being. Article 20(2) prohibits the double jeopardy, which means no one can be punished or tried for the same offence. Article 20(3) provides that no person shall be compelled to be a witness against himself. But this article violated more; a person is tortured to confess against himself in the police station. Article 21 provides for right to life and personal liberty and provides that no person shall be deprived of life and personal liberty except according to procedure established by law. Since torture is an act which affect physically as well as mentally so this is also a related to torture or law against torture. Article 22 provides some guidelines in respect of arrest which must be followed by the person who is arresting. Such as person who is to be arrested should be informed the ground of arrest, should provide right to consult a lawyer of her own choice. Every person arrested should be produce before the magistrate within 24 hours.

5.2.2. under the Indian Penal Code[16], section 220 provides for punishment to an officer or authority that detains or keeps a person in confinement with the corrupt or a malicious motive. Section 330 and 331 provide for punishment of those who inflict injury or grievous hurt on a person to extort confession or information in regard to commission of an offence. Section 330 directly makes the torture punishable under the IPC.

5.2.3. under the Code of Criminal Procedure[17], section 50 provides some rights to the person who is to be arrested and some duties to the person who is arresting. Under section 54 the torture complainant has the right to have medical examination. Section 56 provides that person arrested must be produce before the magistrate without unnecessary delay. Section 57 provides that such arrested person shall not be detain more than the period mentioned in section 167 i.e., 24 hours which is also mentioned under Article 22 of the constitution.

5.2.4. under the Indian Evidence Act[18], section 25 provides that no confession made to the police officer, shall be proved as against a person accused of any offence.

Rapes in police custody are normally seen as stigma on the law enforcing agency by the citizens. Police which is primarily agency for ensuring safety of woman and children, if they themselves get involved in rape cases in police custody. For custodial rape, section 376 of the IPC was amended in 1983[19] and a small change was taking placed, it says an offence of rape committed by a police officer, public servant, a member of a jail or hospital staff on a woman in his custody then he shall be punished with maximum ten years, which seven years for other cases. By this amendment Indian Evidence Act also amended and section 114A was inserted regarding presumption of consent, it says that court shall presumed that woman did not gave her consent in the rape.

5.3. Initiatives taken by Law Commission

The first Law Commission of India (LCI) was appointed in August 1955 and since then eighteen Law Commissions have been appointed and as of 2017, altogether two hundred five reports have been submitted to the Government of India. The issue of admissibility of confession made to senior police officer (a confession recorded by superintendent of police or higher rank should be admissible in court of law) in evidence was taken.[20] However in 2003[21] this subject was examined in great detail and observed that, "it is true, the provisions of certain special Acts dealing with terrorist or organized crime (such as TADA, POTA or MCOCA i.e. Maharashtra Control of Organized Crime Act) contain provisions for recording confessions by and before senior officers of the level of superintendents of Police and for treating them as admissible, subject to certain conditions. Exception made in cases orthopedist should not, in our view, be made applicable to all accused for all types of crimes. That would erode seriously into Article 21 and sections 24 and 25 of the Evidence Act, 1872 and violate article 14. Exception cannot become the rule. In 1989[22] the Law Commission of India suggested a new draft to be added in the Code of Criminal Procedure, 1973, incorporating specific safeguards for the protection of the women in the custody. In 1994[23] Law Commission of India observed that generally the victims of custodial crimes are poor, women, children, disadvantage people and weaker section of the society. The report recommended several changes in the existing laws and procedures including preventive, punitive, compensatory and remedial measures to be inserted in the Indian Penal Code, 1860, Indian Evidence Act, 1872 and code of criminal procedure,1973.The major recommendation of the report was fixation of compensations amount i.e., Rupees 25000 in case of bodily injury and rupees one Lac in case of death. This was an innovative approach of restorative Justice based on individual accountability suggested by the report while dealing with custodial crime. In 2001[24] the Law Commission of India made certain recommendations for safety and wellbeing of detainee in custody of police and also proposed to amend the Cr.P.C, 1973. In 2002[25] the law commission elaborated the right to silence and Article 20(3) of the Constitution of India. It observed that right to silence is a natural corollary of the maxim that no person can be forced to give evidence against him, which is also a part of Article 20.

5.4. Prevention of Torture Bill, 2010

India signed the **Convention against Torture and Other Cruel, Inhuman and Degrading Treatment or Punishment** on October 14, 1997, but not ratified yet. A law needs to be enacted for India to be able to ratify the Convention. The Prevention of Torture Bill, 2010 was introduced in the Lok Sabha on April 26, 2010 by the Minister of Home Affairs, Shri P. Chidambaram to implement such convention under Article 253 of the Constitution. The Bill was passed by the Lok Sabha on May 6, 2010 and is pending in the Rajya Sabha. Then Rajya Sabha referred the bill to the select committee headed by Shri Ashwani Kumar to modify the bill. The committee submitted its report on 6th Dec 2010. The committee accordingly deliberated at length on the various provisions of the bill and also heard the views of cross section of experts and organizations including eminent jurists, academician, civil servants, and members of civil society. The committee notes that the principles and objectives of the bill are to enable India to ratify the "United Nation Convention against Torture and Other Cruel or Degrading Treatment or Punishment" as adopted by the United Nations General Assembly on 9th December, 1975 in order to underscore its irrevocable commitment to the protection and preservation of human rights as guaranteed by the Constitution of India.[26] Then the was Bill lapsed with dissolution of the 15th Lok Sabha following India's refusal to repeal the Armed Forces (Special Powers) Act, 1958 and since then it was never passed. The Prevention of Torture Bill, 2010 seeks to provide for punishment for torture committed by government officials. The Bill defines torture as "grievous hurt", or danger to life, limb and health. Complaints against torture have to be made within six months. The sanction of the appropriate government is required before a court can entertain a complaint.

5.5. Prevention of Torture Bill, 2017:

In May 2017 the NDA Government forwarded the Bill to the Law Commission seeking its comments on the proposed amendments in the IPC. The Law Commission recommended amendments which were necessary for implementation of the UN Convention against torture. The Commission also drafted a bill for the Government to table it in parliament. The draft Bill and the law panel recommendations were submitted to the Government in October 2017 but still it is yet be passed.[27]The Law Commission recommended for stand-alone legislation as well as making consequential amendments in the Cr.P.C, 1973 and the Evidence Act, 1872.[28]

5.6. Failure of Passing Bill:

The torture Bill introduced in the parliament two times one is in 2010 and another is in 2017 but unfortunately till now these Bills are not passed. The 2010 Bill was lapsed due to the dissolution of the house of the parliament; however, it was passed by the lower house and was pending in the upper house and referred to the selection committee. Then in 2014 new Government led by BJP formed and Bill was lapsed. In 2017 also same Bill with some changes introduced but till now not passed. Then Supreme Court issued notice on 22nd Jan 2019 to all the states and UTs to give their opinion regarding the Bill.[29]

5.7. Role of Judiciary:

Judiciary played and playing vital role in protecting the torture in custody but there is a lack of implementation of such order or judgment of Supreme Court. Although under Article 141 the order or judgment made by Supreme Court is binding to all courts and implementation of such order or judgment should be there as like law made by parliament.

If there is any mode of pressure, subtle or crude, mental or physical, direct or indirect, but sufficiently substantial, applied by the police in obtaining information from the accused, it becomes compelled testimony violative of the right against self-incrimination under Article 20(3).[30] Punishment which is too cruel or torturous is unconstitutional.[31]Supreme Court rejected the plea of sovereign immunity and awarded the compensation as the petitioner had been illegally detained in jail for over fourteen years, after his acquittal in full dress trial.[32] Supreme Court issued various directions to protect the custodial violence against female person and arrest thereof in **Sheela Barse V. State of Maharashtra**[33] like to set up separate lock-ups for woman and guarded by female constable, interrogation in the presence female constable etc. It may be legitimate rights of the police to interrogate or arrest any suspect on some credible material but such an arrest must be in accordance with the law and the interrogation does not mean inflicting injuries.[34] Any form of torture or cruel inhuman degrading treatment or punishment is in the purview of Articles 21, 32, 142 and 226 of the Constitution of India.

It is acknowledged remedy. Court has obligation to grant relief formally and finally rejected the defense of sovereign immunity. It also referred Article 9(5) of the International Covenant on Civil and Political Rights.[35]No arrest can be made in a routine manner on a mere allegation of commission of an offence made against a person, it should be prudent of a police officer in the interest of protection of the constitutional rights of a citizens.[36] In **D.K. Basu V. State of West Bengal**[37] Supreme Court initiated the development of custodial jurisprudence including torture to arrestee, infringement of fundamental rights, right to compensation from state and punishment under section 330 of the Indian Penal Code is inadequate to repair the wrong done to citizen. In this case court also provided various guidelines regarding arrest and rights of arrested person, like interrogation of the arrestee must be recorded in a register, the person arrested must be made aware of his rights such to have someone informed regarding his arrest, to choose a lawyer of his own choice, regarding free legal aid etc. Where fundamental rights of the citizens are violated, the plea of sovereign immunity would not available.[38]In spite of such Supreme Court guidelines police continue to detain people without maintaining any record and torture them during such illegal detentions.In **Munshi Singh Gautam V. State of Madhya Pradesh**[39] the Supreme Court took reference of the 135th Report of the Law Commission which has recommended that a section 114-B should be inserted in the Indian Evidence Act, 1872, to introduce a rebuttable resumption that injuries sustained by a person in police custody may be presumed to have been caused by the police officer. Test results of polygraph and brain finger printing tests have been held to be barred by Article 20(3).[40] Accused has right to maintain silence & not to disclose his defense before the trial.[41] Arrest in violation of due procedure seriously jeopardizes the dignity of the person arrested and the law does not continence abuse of power which cause pain and trauma.[42]

5.8. Role of NHRC

National Human Rights Commission established under the **Protection of Human Rights Act**[43] to protect the human rights at national level. This commission recommended the Government of India to ratify the UN Convention against Torture, 1984 various time in order to reduce the cases of torture. Apart from recommendation it develop various practice for combating custodial crimes, such as reporting of custodial death or rape within 24 hours[44], video filming of Post-Mortem examination in case of custodial death[45] , Model autopsy forms and additional procedure for inquest[46], on visit to Police lock-ups, arrest and Polygraph test[47], guidelines to pre-arrest and post-arrest[48], guideline on Polygraph test[49], establishment of Human Rights Cell in State Police Headquarters[50], and establishment of District Complaint Authority[51].

[1] R.S. Saini, *Custodial Torture in law and practice with reference to India*, 36:2 JILI 172 (1994).

[2]*Ibid.*

[3] Mahipal *V.* State of Delhi, 2016 (1) Current Criminal Reports at 117 (Del) (DB), Hanipur Sanji *V.* Khanna and R.K. Gauba, JJ., published from DLT Publications Pvt. Ltd., Delhi.

[4] Chakraborty, p-27.

[5] Kerala Police Reorganizing Police Committee, 1959.

[6] Punjab Police Commission, 1960-61.

[7] Bihar Police Commission, 1961.

[8] West Bengal Police Commission, 1961.

[9] Maharashtra Police Commission, 1964.

[10] Madhya Pradesh Police Commission, 1965.

[11] Delhi Police Commission, 1966-68.

[12]Tamil Nadu Police Commission,1971.

[13] Assam Police Commission, 1971.

[14] First Administration Reform Commission, 1962 Gore Committee on Police Training, 1972.

[15] Observation made by Shah Commission, 1978.

[16] Act No. 45 of 1860, w.e.f. 1st Jan 1862.

[17] Act no 2 of 1974, w.e.f. 1st April 1974.

[18] Act No. 1 of 1872, w.e.f. 1st Sept 1872.

[19] Act No. 43 of 1983, w.e.f. 25th Dec 1983.

[20] 48th Report of Law Commission 1972 and 69th Report of Law commission of India 1977.

[21] 185th Report of law Commission (2003).

[22] 135th Report of Law Commission of India on Women in Custody.

[23] 152nd Report of Law Commission of India on Custodial Crime.

[24] 177th Report of Law Commission of India on Law relating to arrest.

[25] 180th Report of Law Commission of India on Right to silent.

[26] Report of the Select Committee on the Protection of Torture Bill, 2010 headed by Shri Ashwani Kumar (Committee submitted its report to the Upper house of the Parliament on 6th December 2010, and recommended various changes regarding torture law and implementation

of the United Nation Convention against Torture which was also signed by India but not ratified yet).

[27] Read more at: Pradeep Thakur, *Amendment to Prevention of Torture Bill remains in limbo,* Times of India (Aug 22, 2022) https://timesofindia.indiatimes.com/india/amendment-to-prevention-of-torture-bill-remains-in-limbo/articleshow/65202546.cms

[28]273rd Report of the Law Commission of India, 2017, (submitted its report to the Government in October 2017), The commission recommended followings:

(i) Ratification of Convention against Torture-In order to tide over the difficulties faced by the Country in getting criminals extradited, in the absence of an anti-torture law and to secure an individual's right to life and liberty, the Commission recommended consideration of the Convention Against Torture for ratification and in the event, the Central Government decides to ratify the Convention, then the draft Bill might be considered.

(ii) Amendment to Existing Statutes-The Commission came to the conclusion that the Criminal Procedure Code, 1973 and the Indian Evidence Act, 1872 require amendments to accommodate provisions regarding compensation and burden of proof, respectively.

a. Criminal Procedure Code, 1973: The Commission recommended amendment to section 357B to incorporate payment of compensation, in addition to payment of fine, as provided under section 326A or section 376D of the Indian Penal Code, 1860.

b. Indian Evidence Act, 1872: The Commission endorses the recommendation made by the Law Commission of India that the Indian Evidence Act, 1872 requires insertion of Section 114B as insertion of this section must ensure that in case a person in police custody sustains injuries, it is presumed that those injuries have been inflicted by the police, and the burden of proof shall lie on the authority concerned to explain such injury.

(iii) Punishment for acts of torture-In order to curb the menace of torture and to have a deterrent effect on acts of torture, the Commission recommended stringent punishment to the perpetrators of such acts thereby proposing in a draft Bill the term for punishment extending up to life imprisonment and fine.

(iv) Compensation policy for Victims-According to the Law Commission's recommendations, the Courts would decide upon a justiciable compensation after taking into account various facets of an individual case, such as nature, purpose, extent and manner of injury, including mental agony caused to the victim. The Courts would also bear in mind the socio-economic background of the victim and will ensure that the compensation so decided will suffice the victim to bear the expenses on medical treatment and rehabilitation.

(v) Protection of Victims, Complainants and Witnesses-The Commission recommended that an effective mechanism must be put in place in order to protect the victims of torture, the complainants and the witnesses against possible threats, violence or ill treatment.

(vi) Sovereign Immunity-Going by the law of torts, which states 'liability follows negligence' the Commission was of the opinion that the State should own the responsibility for the injuries caused by its agents on citizens, and principle of sovereign immunity cannot override the rights assured by the Constitution. While dealing with the plea of sovereign immunity, the Courts will have to bear in mind that it is the citizens who are entitled for fundamental rights, and not the agents of the State.

[29]Gaurav Vivek Bhatnagar, *SC Directs All States, UTs to Send Replies on Torture Bill Within Three Weeks*, the Wire (Aug 13, 2022) https://thewire.in/law/sc-directs-all-states-uts-to-send-replies-on-torture-bill-within-three-weeks

[30] Nadini Satpati *V.* P.L. Dhani, AIR 1978 SCC 1075.

[31] Inderjit Singh *V.* State of Uttar Pradesh, AIR 1979 SC 1867.

[32] Rudal Shah *V.* State of Bihar, AIR 1983 SC 1086.

[33] AIR 1983 SC 378.

[34] Bhagwan Singh *V.* State of Punjab, (1992) 3 SCC 249.

[35] Nilabati Behara *V.* State of Orissa, AIR 1993 SC 1960.

[36] Joginder Kumar *V.* State of Uttar Pradesh, (1994) 4 SCC 260: AIR 1994 SC 1349.

[37] (1997) 1 SCC 416: AIR 1997 SC 610.

[38] State of Andhra Pradesh *V.* Challa Ramakrishna Reddy, AIR 2000 SC 2083.

[39] AIR 2005 SC 631.

[40] Smt. Selvi *V.* State of Karnataka, AIR 2010 SC 1974.

[41] Yogendra Kumar Jaiswal *V.* State of Bihar, AIR 2016 SC 1474.

[42] Dr. Rini JOhar *V.* State of Madhya Pradesh, AIR 2016 SC 2679.

[43] Act 10 of 1994, w.e.f. 28th September 1993.

[44] 14th December 1993.

[45] 10th August 1995.

[46] 27th March 1997.

[47] 1st August 1997.
[48] 22nd November 1999.
[49] 11th January 2000.
[50] 2nd August 1999.
[51] 24th December 1999.

CHAPTER SIX

CONCLUSION

In India mostly the torture is perpetuated by the police, jail authorities, armed forces and other law enforcing authorities, however to regulate such torture there are enough number of laws exists but there is only lack of implementation of such laws. As discussed above from constitution of India to other enactment and from Law Commission to Supreme Court all are played vital role in providing the law against torture, still there are various events regarding torture in police custody or judicial custody. India needs to pass a separate law on torture because India needs effective implementation of law on torture, and now in the present-day India having provisions against torture not in one document rather in various documents so it is very difficult to implement such law effectively. For example, in **D.K. Basu case** Supreme Court order issued some guidelines regarding arrest and interrogation and also directed all the States and Centre to make advertise such guidelines through radio and television but till date no such awareness or advertisement made either by State or by the Centre. So, in order make effective implementation it should make separate legislation on custodial torture with effective punishment.

As of June 2021, The UN Convention against Torture 1984, has 171 state parties. If we talk about the BRICS members except India all other four members signed and ratified the convention, but India only signed it on 14th October 1997 yet not ratified till date. Brazil signed the Convention on 23rd September 1985 and ratified on 28th September 1989, Russia signed it on 10th December 1985 and ratified on 3rd March 1987, China signed it on 12th December 1986 and ratified on 4th October 1988, South Africa signed it on 29th June 1993 and ratified on 10th Dec 1998. The country like India which is the largest democracy in the world should ratify the Convention as soon as possible not only because its common group member already signed and ratified it but for the respects India has for human rights. With regard to the separate legislation on torture law, among BRICS members Brazil and South Africa having specific legislation to prevent and combat torture. Brazil passed a federal law in 2015 that established a National System to Prevent and Combat Torture and South Africa passed *the Prevention of Combatting and Torture of Persons Act, 2013*. Russia and China having their own domestic law to prevent and combat torture. India also having its own domestic law in various documents such as Constitution, 1950, Indian Penal Code, 1860, Indian Evidence Act, 1872, Criminal Procedure Code, 1973 etc. but such laws are not effective due to the absence of the enforcement mechanism, So India need to pass a separate legislation on torture like its co-member of BRICS group Brazil and South Africa passed for the same.

www.ingramcontent.com/pod-product-compliance
Lightning Source LLC
Chambersburg PA
CBHW050818160726
48004CB00002B/909